# A BAD START IN LIFE - CHILDREN, HEALTH AND HOUSING
## BY ANNETTE FURLEY

*"... a good start in life can bring years of happiness and fulfillment over a whole lifespan."*

■

Sir Douglas Black, author of the Black Report

1

## FOREWORD

Children are very rarely included in discussions about housing policies.

Like women and people from black and ethnic minority communities, the needs of children are hidden. They do not even appear in the statistics.

Such an approach not only presents a partial view of housing needs, it devalues children - who are human beings with their own human rights.

The aim of this report is to highlight the terrible and sometimes fatal effects on children's health of bad housing and homelessness and it begins the process of putting children firmly in the housing picture.

It reveals how Britain's housing crisis is hitting hardest those who are the most vulnerable, those with the least political power and shows the importance of housing policy on the physical, mental and emotional development of children.

It also reminds us that children, whose voices so often go unheard, have a right to a decent home - one of the most basic human needs - if they are to have any sort of reasonable start in life.

The type of home a child has can in part determine their start in life - yet the quality and quantity of housing rarely acknowledges this fact.

For those without permanent accommodation, life can be particularly tough.

Some 30,000 children are growing up in rooms often no larger than 12' x 18'. Learning to walk in the gap between the bed and wall is no fun for the parent. It is no fun for the children either.

And its getting worse. Since 1979 the numbers of homeless families forced to live in temporary accommodation have increased ten fold with many families having to stay for between 18 months to five years.

In areas where homeless people used to get permanent housing the tendency now is for them to be placed in hostels or bed and breakfast hotels.

Throughout Britain childhood can mean growing up in conditions with which Victorian health inspectors would be at home.

The quality and quantity of housing is firmly in decline. More people are unable to live in decent conditions today than at any time since the 1950s.

Britain's housing stock is ageing. Houses produced in large numbers around the turn of the century are all getting old together, contributing to a need for more investment in major repair and modernisation work.

But since 1979 housing has borne the brunt of public spending cuts. Housing's share of public money has fallen from ten to two per cent of total government spending. Today, councils are allowed to borrow only a quarter of what they were able to get five years ago.

The government estimates that over 900,000 homes are unfit for human habitation. A further 900,000 people - many of whom are children - are living in extreme overcrowding. More and more, children are living on the top floors of tower blocks as councils find their supply of maisonettes and houses dries up.

The lack of investment has produced new slums with flats inadequately heated, kitchens and bathrooms too small to cater for adults and children.

As for the building of new homes, in 1988 15,000 council homes were completed compared with 100,000 in the mid 1970s. Housing associations also experienced a drop from 19,000 completions in 1980 to just 9,000 last year.

Houses are the best sellers under the Governments 'Right to Buy' scheme introduced a decade ago. A national survey of tenants and buyers of council homes carried out by the Department of the Environment last year showed that 56% of homes bought were semi- detached houses and only 3% were flats and maisonettes.

For the first time since the second World War, homes for rent are in a real decline at a time when demand has never been so great. This loss, coupled with the lack of new homes, has particularly hit families with children who are increasingly condemned to live for years in poor and overcrowded conditions.

And there's worse to come. The combined effects of the Housing Act 1988 and the new Local Government and Housing Bill are likely to increase the cost of accommodation while reducing its quality and quantity still further. Rising housing costs will hit poorer families in particular who find it impossible to make ends meet as rents go through the roof. The poll tax will add extra costs to family budgets when it comes into operation in England in 1990.

The lack of affordable rented accommodation particularly in the public sector is going to disproportionately affect those families on the waiting list and those trying to move to more suitable council or housing association accommodation. The appalling conditions which political parties of all persuasions fought and won elections campaigning against are now returning to haunt the lives of new generations.

Children's housing needs are both separate and inter-linked with those of adults. Their living conditions are not of their own choosing yet they have distinctive needs which are unlikely to be met under the current housing priorities. That's why Shelter firmly believes that we need to re-think the principles on which housing policies are based.

*ALAN BOOTH, Shelter Campaigns Organiser.*

900,000 homes are unfit for human habitation. 900,000 people - many of whom are children - are living in extreme overcrowding .

(English House Conditions Survey 1986, DoE HMSO 1988)

# CONTENTS

2 | FOREWORD

3 | THE HOUSING CRISIS

6 | INTRODUCTION

8 | WHAT IS A HOME?

10 | HEALTH AND HOUSING

11 | MENTAL HEALTH

14 | RESPIRATORY PROBLEMS

16 | INFECTIOUS DISEASES

17 | MORTALITY

18 | DISABILITY

19 | PLAY AND DEVELOPMENT

22 | SAFETY

25 | BED AND BREAKFAST AND HOSTEL ACCOMMODATION

29 | ACCESS TO HEALTH CARE

32 | RACISM

34 | TRAVELLERS

35 | RUNAWAYS

36 | CONCLUSION

38 | TOWARDS A BETTER START IN LIFE

40 | SOURCES

In the late 1980s, it is outrageous that a report like this is still needed.

Children continue to live in appalling, overcrowded conditions, often little better than in the last century. They are living in damp, cold flats, houses that are dangerous or hostels and hotels unfit even for the hardiest of adults. Many live in rooms which they share with several other people with no washing, cooking or play facilities.

Children in poorer families suffer most. Poverty is a major barrier to good housing. Children from wealthier families do not live in poor housing.

But perhaps the most frightening aspect is the long-term effects that inadequate living conditions may be having on these children's health - generating future adults with potentially avoidable health, social and emotional problems.

Poor housing may be contributing to forms of ill-health not apparent until later years. Increased incidence of hospital admission and higher mortality and morbidity in later life have already been associated with poor housing in childhood. (1,2)

Poor housing plays a significant part in the cycle of deprivation: a low income* can mean no escape, feelings of low self-esteem, reduced motivation, ill-health.

In housing as in other areas, children's needs have been neglected. It seems that existing research has not been enough to shame governments into taking the housing crisis seriously, even for the sake of our children's well-being. Significantly, the government's current health service review does not address the issue of housing and health.

If policy-makers are not moved by the fact that children's basic right to good health is being denied, they may be persuaded by economic arguments. Through under-resourcing housing now, huge extra resources will be needed to cope with the increased health and social problems caused by poor housing and homelessness.

## One fifth of children in Britain are living on the poverty line.

(Child Poverty Action Group - from government statistics, 1985)

---

*Low Income: More than nine million adult workers - about 44% of the workforce - earn less than the Low Pay Unit's definition of low wages (of £132.27 for a basic 37.5 hour week). Of these, five million were working full-time and four million part-time. (The Poor Decade, Wage Inequalities in the 1980s; Low Pay Unit, 1988)*

*Poverty: In Britain in 1985, 15,420,000 were living in or on the margins of poverty (140% of supplementary benefit level or below) - 29% of the population. (Poverty The Facts. Child Poverty Action Group, 1988)*

Good housing is of such great importance to the whole of our lives. A home allows us to develop as human beings, to acquire confidence in social skills, to maintain good health and at some point to feel safe and protected, to grow towards independence.

Anthea Holme (3) found that the majority of parents thought of a home as "somewhere to be on their own," with very simple criteria for an ideal home, such as somewhere to relax, a garden and a specific locality. Those who were most content in their housing were those with the greatest security.

Morris Schaefer (4) feels that "... at best our dwellings promote emotional and social health by providing psychological security, physical ties with ones community and cultures and a means to express ones individuality."

But perhaps the definition which best sums up what a home is comes from the Faith in the City report (5) : "A house is more than bricks and mortar, it is more than a roof over ones head. Decent housing is a place that is dry and warm and in reasonable repair. It also means security, privacy, sufficient space; a place where people can grow, make choices, become more whole people. It relates to the environment in which the house is located."

Unfortunately, too many children cannot say they have such a home.

The World Health Organisation defines health as "a state of complete physical, mental and social well-being and not merely an absence of disease or infirmity."

There are several reports, studies and papers concerned with the effects of housing and the environment on the health of the population.

The Black Report (6), Court Report (7) and Whitehead Report (8) all describe the relationship between disadvantage, class and health, poor housing or homelessness often being inseparably linked with that disadvantage.

It is difficult to disentangle the effects of housing from the effects of other socio-economic factors such as class, income and poverty. But many studies have highlighted the correlations and others have found a clear relationship. The Black Report found that there was a relationship between tenure type and health, with homeowners faring better than other households because of increased space and security.

Morris Schaefer felt that conditions of dwellings in inner city slums put women's and children's health particularly at risk. The Court Report agrees that among those whose health is particularly vulnerable are children living in poor housing or who are considered homeless.

Many children may even be dying because of the environment they live in. Though there is still much speculation, an unsuitable environment may be a contributory factor in some of the 1,500 plus Sudden Infant Deaths that occur each year (9).

Homes should provide protection from health hazards but in a much more positive sense they should also be environments which promote good health. All studies acknowledge that good housing is essential in order to achieve good health. Over and over again, they suggest that there will be positive effects when the housing is good, but in poor conditions, the effects will be the reverse. This sounds like common sense but Britain's housing policies do not always take this simple equation into account.

Steve Morton (10) states: "Housing is integral to public health ..."

*"Politicians must realise that housing and health are not separate issues."*

■

Sonja Hunt, Edinburgh University Research Unit in health and behavioural change, 1988

## A BAD START IN LIFE - MARK ■

**The D family are a young couple with two children aged five and two and a half.**

**They have been living in a hotel for 9 months, sharing the kitchen with 32 other families.**

**Five-year-old Mark has behavioural problems and is having a lot of trouble at school. In particular, he refuses to join in classroom discussions about what the children do on holidays or at weekends.**

**Says his mother: "On one occasion he got very, very tearful and just started vomiting in the school for no reason. He's closing in on himself. He can't understand why he hasn't got a home of his own when all the other children have homes."**

The mental health of children and their parents is so often closely intertwined.

Children are sensitive to the moods of their carers and a child exposed to a parent depressed about their living conditions will undoubtedly be affected.

A depressed mother who is breast feeding may find her milk dries up; a parent out of work because of their problematic housing situation may become frustrated and take his or her aggression out on the children; a whole family living in one room are likely to affect each others mental state, with no privacy, constant noise and no space for the children to play. A British Medical Journal article discusses the affect of constant noise from others in overcrowded accommodation (11).

Adults in poor housing are often overwhelmed with feelings of powerlessness to which children will be sensitive. Older children in particular will be aware of the stigma so often associated with poor living conditions or the label of homelessness.

The adverse relationship between a poor environment and health, behaviour and school achievement has been well documented. Rutter and Madge (12) highlighted the negative effects on children's behaviour and emotional state caused by being homeless or in poor housing, as well as the increased degree of educational failure.

Other studies make similar findings as well as showing the effects of living in certain urban environments. Freeman (13) demonstrated links between living in highrise flats or on run-down estates with some psychiatric conditions. A North Manchester Health Authority report (14) supports these findings showing that the mental health of adults improves when they move out of tower blocks.

More recent research from Edinburgh University (15) shows that children living in environments internally polluted by damp and mould are more likely to experience poor educational and intellectual performance as well as suffering more emotional distress.

### A BAD START IN LIFE - MICHELLE ■

Eighteen-month-old Michelle lives with her parents in a late Victorian brick-built terraced house.

She was a healthy baby despite the privately-rented house being very damp and in chronic disrepair.

But a year ago the ancient coal-fired heating system broke down and began leaking dangerous fumes. Despite repeated attempts, the parents could not persuade the landlord to repair it.

They were left with a choice - suffer the poisonous fumes or turn the heating off completely in the middle of winter. They decided to turn the heating off but by that time Michelle had developed severe respiratory problems and she has little chance of making a full recovery while living in such a cold, damp environment.

Respiratory infections are the most common cause of death in children between the ages of one and 14 years (16).

For many years, health professionals have argued whether damp really causes respiratory problems. It is generally accepted that asthma is often exacerbated by poor housing conditions (17,18,19). As with so many other illnesses, asthma may also be aggravated by the effects of stress caused by living in these same conditions.

Recent research from Edinburgh University (15), however, appears to confirm that children living in damp conditions are more likely to suffer respiratory problems such as persistent coughs, wheezes, runny noses and are more susceptible to infections causing fevers, sore throats and headaches. The housing studied had poor ventilation and heating, contributing to mould and damp.

This study is perhaps one of the most important in relating poor health to poor housing as, unlike many others, it has taken into account most other variables such as low income, overcrowding and smoking. However, it does support the findings of earlier research. Strachman (16) found an association between respiratory problems reported by parents and damp, mouldy housing. McCarthy et al's (20) research suggests a similar correlation and the

Department of the Environment study in 1981 (21) concluded that unsatisfactory housing was contributing to high rates of respiratory disease, aggravated by ducted warm air heating and the practice of drying clothes indoors because of inadequate laundry facilities.

This is a clear example of a situation in which children's health could be greatly improved by better standards of housing. It is estimated that 2 million homes in Britain suffer from severe dampness and a further 2.5 million suffer some degree of dampness (6).

Ironically, some instances of houses being chemically treated for damp have resulted in breathing difficulties, skin disorders and stomach and chest pains (22).

Five hundred and thirteen children were taken into care in 1986 because the families were homeless.

Parliamentary Questions, 1988

It is generally accepted that overcrowding is an important factor in the spread of infectious disease, yet so many children continue to live in extremely overcrowded conditions. With the dramatic increase in the number of families now living in hotel accommodation, a number of organisations, including the Health Visitors' Association, have been drawing attention to this issue.

Reports and studies are constantly highlighting the problem. One of the most recent, produced jointly by Shelter, SHAC, the Maternity Alliance and the London Food Commission (23), shows definitively that children living in hotel accommodation are at increased risk.

Children living in close proximity with many others will more readily catch viruses, respiratory infections and diseases such as chicken pox. This is particular worrying in the case of children living in temporary accommodation who may also have decreased access to health services for immunisation and other preventative care.

Dr Sue Jenkins (24) writes that "in what can only be termed as a depriving environment, acute infections both viral and bacterial are common and quick to spread in overcrowded conditions."

The spread of infectious diseases is also aided by the lack of basic amenities such as running water, good sanitary facilities, adequate rubbish disposal and hygienic food storage and preparation areas. Too many properties in Britain are still without some of these basic requirements.

### A BAD START IN LIFE - JOANNA ■

**The A family are a couple, both aged 20, sharing a small room in a hotel with their eight-month-old daughter Joanna.**

**Until Mrs A could get a place for her daughter in a toddlers' group, Joanna spent most of the day in the room except for shopping trips.**

**She began to have prolonged screaming fits and was referred to a child psychologist who believed confinement to the room was upsetting her.**

**"Last week Joanna was very bad," said Mrs A. "The screaming started again and I took her to the doctor's and he couldn't understand. She started getting sick in the night, two nights ago she got sick. And then in the morning she had diarrhoea, the kids they all get it."**

Poor housing can be associated with a number of indicators of mortality (6).

It is families with children, especially large poor families, who are most likely to be living in overcrowded conditions.

Brennan and Lancashire (25) found a clear correlation between overcrowding and an increased mortality rate among 0-4 year olds and a significant correlation in 5-15 year olds. Other studies (8,26,27) have found a similar relationship between overcrowding and increased death rates, particularly during the perinatal period.

And there is more than a suspicion that a poor environment may contribute to the high rate of Sudden Infant Deaths in this country (9).

As the housing crisis worsens, many local authorities are putting fewer resources into converting accommodation to meet the needs of families with children with disabilities. Some are also giving medical points a lower priority for rehousing. This may mean that the children have to live in institutions as families cannot look after them at home.

Alternatively, trying to manage in unsuitable accommodation can cause stress and related illnesses and in some cases, conditions can exacerbate the child's disability.

Children with severe chest problems may be at increased risk because of damp or inadequate heating. Children with mobility difficulties will be hindered by too many stairs or inappropriately sized lifts: sometimes children become virtual prisoners in their own homes. Families with incontinent children and the children themselves will be further burdened if there is nowhere to dry clothes and linen or if they have to share a bed because of overcrowding.

Although there seems to be little research looking specifically at the relationship between children with disabilities and poor housing, related research suggests a significant association (28).

### A BAD START IN LIFE - PETER ■

**Eight-year-old Peter has cerebral palsy. He has little speech and very little use of his legs. He lives with his parents and two brothers in a small housing association flat which is due for renovation.**

**A physiotherapist has tried to encourage Peter to walk with the aid of a frame but because of the lack of space, he spends most of his time shuffling around the flat on his bottom.**

**The conditions in the flat add to the problems. It is infested by cockroaches and mice. And getting Peter to the outside toilet requires an enormous amount of patience and effort.**

**Peter is also incontinent but he has to share a bed with his brothers because of overcrowding. Sheets and clothes have to be washed constantly but the flat is so damp, it is impossible to dry or air anything properly.**

Play is essential to any child's development and yet so many children are hindered by a lack of space or excessive exposure to environmental risks. Children need an environment which makes play possible, safe and stimulating.

The Department of the Environment (29) have stated that: "It is important that family housing be designed with the needs of children uppermost. Multi-storey buildings are generally unsuitable for families with young children ... estates as a whole therefore have to be designed with play habits in mind and play spaces carefully located..."

Despite such unambiguous reports, many local authorities have found it necessary to abandon policies whereby families with children are not placed in accommodation above the fourth floor.

All too often, estates' play facilities have been shut down due to lack of funds to maintain them. Many areas have no play facilities in the first place. This is particularly damaging for families living in highrise blocks or in hotel accommodation.

All this is in the face of the widely accepted and well publicised fact that the role of play in a child's development is absolutely vital. Tony Chiltern (30) points out that where there are cold, unimaginative, stark and aggressive physical features in an environment, children's play behaviour will be unimaginative, stark and physically aggressive.

Environmental psychologists stress playful interaction with the environment as essential in the learning process. But many children are denied this interaction. The Black Report reinforces findings in studies that show that tower block life is damaging for children. One particular study in Denmark (31) makes several telling points:

■ children in highrise flats have greater contact difficulties and fewer contacts with friends
■ children in tower blocks go out to play independently at a later age than other children
■ these children have a shorter period of outdoor play
■ the high density population in these areas often results in increased conflicts and stress in children's play

Living in bed and breakfast accommodation for long periods has been observed to adversely affect children's development. Reports by the Health Visitors' Association, Shelter and the Community Paediatrics Research Unit all show that children's behaviour is affected and development delayed.

Children living in small, overcrowded or poorly designed accommodation with their families have no space to develop motor skills or to learn to explore or interact with others in games.

An unsafe environment and lack of privacy all contribute to children's behavioural problems and

19

delayed speech and walking abilities. The severity of the problems appear to be related to the amount of time a family spends in an unsuitable environment.

## SOME POSITIVE INITIATIVES

In Newcastle, the work between the Recreation and Leisure and City Planning departments has ensured that all future housing developments will include appropriate levels of informal and formal play provision. This is now an enforceable city council policy.

There are a few local authorities, such as Middlesborough, Halifax and Bristol, who still adhere to their policy of not placing families with children in high level tower blocks.

**Sixty-one per cent of households accepted as homeless have children.**

Court Report, 1984

## A BAD START IN LIFE - THE KHATUN/MIAH FAMILY ■

The Khatun/Miah family, originally from Bangladesh, consists of Mum, Dad and six children, aged from one to eleven years.

When their first flat was demolished, they were moved to a damp, draughty flat with only two bedrooms and situated next to two busy, noisy roads.

The mother quickly became very depressed, suffering from sleeplessness and nightmares. The children are constantly ill with coughs and colds due to the cold, damp conditions and stressful lifestyle.

The eight-year-old has also developed problems at school, the six-year-old suffers from terrible rashes and the five-year-old is not eating or sleeping properly.

Fights between the children break out frequently and all of them have suffered accidents in the home because of lack of space and proper facilities.

The Khatun/Miah family have been told for five years now that they will be moved as soon as possible.

Each year about 250,000 children are admitted to hospital following an accident involving architectural features in the home (32).

Under any circumstances, children have accidents because of the nature of their development of which exploration is a vital component. But the majority of house-related accidents could be eliminated by better design and improved repair services.

Deaths as a result of accidents now account for about one third of all childhood mortalities and although the majority of these are due to road accidents, fire and drowning, most accidents in the under five age group occur in or near the home. Working class children who are more likely to be living in areas without safe play space are between five and seven times more likely than some other children to be hit by a car (33).

A recent study in the London borough of Haringey (34) shows that 72% of injuries in the under five age group were sustained in accidents at home. The study also shows that the number of accidents is higher in areas of deprivation and where there are increased indicators of poverty.

Children living in overcrowded hotel accommodation are particularly at risk from fire and falls. Thirty per cent of multi-occupied buildings lack satisfactory means of escape from fire (35). Thirty-three per cent of houses in multiple occupation (HMOs) need major

repairs (35). Many falls are caused by ill-fitting railings and bannisters and broken window catches.

Burns and scalds from kettles, cooking rings and electric fires are also very common because of lack of space.

Other reports highlighting the problems include one by the Thomas Coram Foundation for Children (36) and a joint survey by the Health Visitors' Association and Shelter (37).

"My daughter has been scalded and other children have had electric shocks. In your own home, you can be careful, have gates across doorways and so on but in a hotel, you've got to put up with other people's carelessness." (Arlene, Speaking Out, Bayswater Hotel Homelessness Project, 1987).

In 1983, 128,000 children up to 14 years old suffered falls and burns in the home. There were another 45,000 accidents in the outdoor area involving children falling on hard surfaces or fences. And accidents involving glass in windows and doors numbered 42,500 in the same year (38).

Children's safety in the home is not only a question of accident prevention. Our homes should provide protection against all risks to health but many houses are themselves  health hazards.

Poor sanitary facilities are a risk to children's health. So too is exposure to asbestos and lead in older houses although the effects of these hazards have as yet been poorly researched.

Allergy expert Dr Mumby (39) feels that new homes are often no safer because of the chemicals used in modern systems.  He believes that toxic substances used in certain paints, bathroom fittings and carpets can be the underlying cause of some rashes, migraines and depressions.

Certainly, treatments used to combat rot and woodworm have been shown to cause a number of health problems.  Poisoning, through  skin contact, inhalation and ingestion leading to nausea, respiratory problems, headaches and depression, has followed the use of chemicals for home preservation. (40)

Problems caused by the chemicals, glare and flickering of fluorescent lighting have also been documented, ranging from headaches, irritation, tiredness, lack of concentration and eye strain to hyper-activity and epileptic fits. This lighting is still being used in some buildings, despite Health and Safety Executive warnings and guidelines (41).

*POSITIVE INITIATIVE*

The National Tower Block Network received a DoE grant for research, and now run training sessions, on safety in the home for tenants and local authority officers.

Over 11,000 households are living in temporary accommodation and the detrimental effects on health of living in bed and breakfast hotels have been well documented (24,36,37,42). One particularly alarming report (23) shows that pregnant women who are homeless are three times more likely to be admitted to hospital and more likely to have underweight and premature babies.

Generally, conditions in hotel accommodation for homeless people are appalling and totally unsuitable for family life.

Privacy is virtually non-existent; marital disputes can increase, children have nowhere to do their homework and high levels of stress often lead to increased incidence of non-accidental injury.

Lack of space and reduced motivation can severely delay children's development. Walking and speech problems are particularly common.

Children living in hotels are also more likely to have behavioural and emotional problems.

It may be difficult for them to get into regular patterns of sleep with the whole family living in one room and often having to share beds.

As discussed earlier, children are more likely to suffer accidents in this environment.

Standards of hygiene are difficult to maintain when nappies have to be washed in the same sink as hands or food because of lack of facilities. It is no surprise that infectious diseases spread so rapidly. One research project in progress in hotels and the casualty department within Parkside Health Authority is showing that children living in hotels are three times more likely than other children to get gastroenteritis (43).

Nutritional standards are also difficult to maintain. Hotels offer inadequate cooking facilities and storage space so that families are often forced to rely on take-aways which are expensive and not always nutritionally sound. Hotel living can be generally very expensive and families are known to go short of food.

In addition, families whose diets are governed by their religion can have major problems because of lack of proper facilities and the provision of traditional English breakfasts by hotels.

Depressed mothers may find that it is difficult to breast feed. Lack of facilities to sterilise bottles lead to an increased risk of gastric infections.

Steve Morton's report found that previously homeless families felt that their stay in temporary accommodation had had a long term effect on their health. (44)

## SOME POSITIVE INITIATIVES

The Bayswater Hotel Homelessness Project was set up in 1984 to advise families living in hotels in the area. The project also undertakes research and provides information for campaigning as well as acting as a pressure group. They host the Bayswater Co-ordinating Group which involves various voluntary and statutory bodies looking at ways of working together for the benefit of homeless families.

The Bayswater Parents and Under Fives Group was also established in 1984 as a space where families could escape some of the pressures of hotel living. As well as toys and play facilities for children, it provides a friendly atmosphere, a place to relax, meet others, cook and participate in group activities. The families themselves have set up a campaigning group to highlight the conditions they have to endure and to fight for homes.

Field Lane Centre in London run a drop-in centre with play facilities and playgroup, a meeting place, cooking and laundry facilities. The workers are also available to give advice, visit hotels and support residents groups.

Hopscotch is an Asian Family Centre funded by Save the Children. Many hotel homeless people in London are of Asian origin and Hopscotch offers a drop-in centre as well as organised pick ups of families from hotels. Many families are fearful of leaving their hotels because of racial harassment. This project gets them out and into a safe environment where they can play, cook, learn English and get advice.

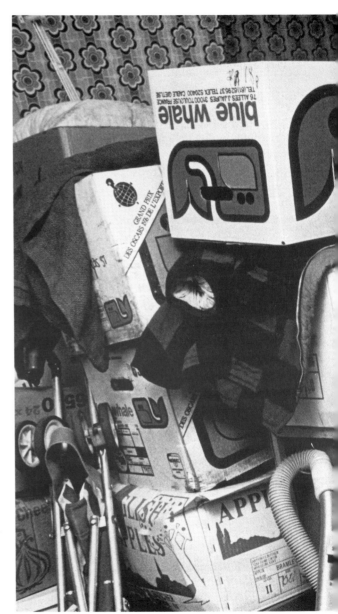

*"The health of the children must come first. How can you keep healthy in a place like this, which we all accept is not a good environment."*

■

Hotel proprietor, Bed and Breakfast Report,
Valerie Howarth

### A BAD START IN LIFE - THE JOHNSON TWINS ■

These year old twins have been diagnosed as having diabetes. They share one hotel room with their sister and mother.

The hotel facilities do not include a private fridge where the insulin, syringes and needles can be kept safe.

There are also limited cooking facilities which make catering for the children's special diet difficult.

Due to the overcrowding, the twins are at high risk of accidents and infection which can be particularly dangerous for children with diabetes. Stress makes the condition more difficult to control.

## A BAD START IN LIFE - CHILDREN OF THE BRICKYARD COTTAGES ■

**The Brickyard Cottages are a row of 12 former pit houses in Nottinghamshire used by Broxtowe Borough Council to house homeless families and described by one housing aid worker in the area as 'the punishment block.'**

**The site is very isolated, up a narrow, unlit, unmade lane in the middle of the countryside and a mile from the nearest main road.**

**The colliery and brickyard which used to be there are now derelict. Old buildings, potholes, broken glass, pieces of wood and all sorts of debris like asbestos make this, says Simon Alvey of Shelter Nottingham, "an extraordinarily dangerous place for children."**

**The housing itself gives rise to health problems among the children - it is poor quality and constantly damp. And its isolation makes it difficult for families to get the health care they need. The nearest health centre is miles away and it's very difficult to get doctors to visit the Cottages.**

**The isolation also has implications for the children's schooling. The nearest school being almost three miles away, the children - some as young as 7 or 8 and until recently, one epileptic boy - have to travel on their own by public transport.**

Inequalities in the use of health services appear to be greatest in the case of preventative services.

It is difficult to separate out access to services, under provision and under usage but it is clear that poorer groups make relatively low use of GP services and more use of casualty departments (6).

The Black Report suggests that this may be due principally to the greater availability of accident and emergency departments but it may also be because people feel they will find a better quality service.

Skrimshire's report (45) is concerned with the lack of provision in different localities. The study states: "A working class person is at greater disadvantage if he (sic) lives in a predominantly working class area than if he lives in a socially mixed one."

West and Lowe (46) found a connection between the low provision of GPs and health visitors in certain areas and a high incidence of stillbirth and infant mortality. A relationship has also been found with poor housing in such areas. The different factors are so intertwined, generally suggesting that people living in inadequate housing (and hence with increased mortality and morbidity rates) are also those less likely to have access to the health care they so desperately need.

Professor Neville Butler (47) found that standards of housing, availability of transport and education of parents are important factors in the take up of services. For example, those children already disadvantaged are less likely to have had immunisation.

Families living in hotel accommodation are likely to have increased health needs but their access to health services is limited (24,36,37,42,44).

Due to a lack of resources and the stigma attached to homelessness, families often experience problems registering with GPs.

Other health care workers are often under-resourced particularly in areas of high density population. This coupled with poor systems of communication about families' placement, means that many children miss out entirely on basic health care.

Homeless or badly housed children are likely to have immunisations and development assessments late, if at all, and where ongoing treatment is required, it may be disrupted or in some instances, it may stop altogether.

Families' use of casualty departments is often inappropriate. One ambulanceman in the Bayswater area of London pointed out that a large number of calls from people in bed and breakfast accommodation are unnecessary but they often have no alternative.

Families in other forms of temporary accommodation are often placed in areas some distance from their social support networks. Families whose first language is not English may be accommodated in areas where there are few, if any, health workers who speak their language, no interpreters and little if any understanding of their culture. Even if local services are well resourced, they may not be meeting families' needs.

## SOME POSITIVE INITIATIVES

Many families living in hotels do not attend health clinics for a variety of reasons. At Finsbury Park in London, a mobile health clinic for homeless families operates one day a week.

The Bayswater Care Team consists of health and social services professionals working together with families, providing clinic and visiting sessions. The team work very closely with voluntary agencies in the area in providing health care.

Money has recently been allocated from the Kings Fund for a new project in Bayswater. GPs in the area felt that they were not providing an adequate service for homeless families. The Bayswater GP surgery distributes the work among 21 GPs, offering continuity of care for those who need it. Families now have access to a GP who is aware of the particular effects on health of hotel living.

A scheme in the London Borough of Tower Hamlets has taken the clinic and health sessions into an area of very poor housing where occupants of temporary accommodation were under using the health centre facilities. The clinic/community room has been taken on site to make access easier in an attempt to improve immunisation rates and uptake of developmental assessments.

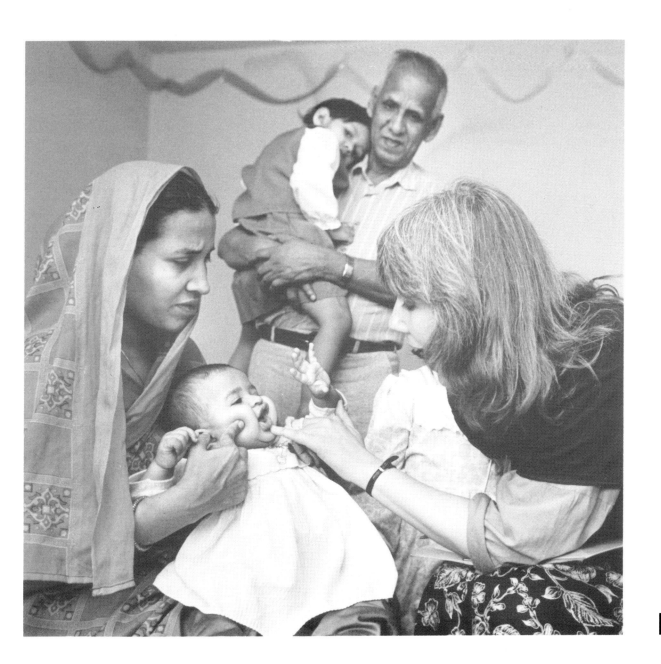

## A BAD START IN LIFE - GURDEEP ■

**Bhavani and her two sons, aged 12 and 6, were hoping to make a fresh start in a new area.**

**But after a couple of weeks, some of the neighbours on their new estate began to abuse and harass the family, explicitly because of their Asian origin.**

**The problems continued at school. Twelve-year-old Gurdeep was regularly called names, threatened, bullied and beaten up. He began to disappear for periods of up to two or three days at a time and the effect on his school-work was disastrous. He finally told his mother he was too frightened to return to their flat or to the school.**

**The local council took no action against the harassers but agreed to transfer the family.**

Racism is an unacceptable part of our society but it is a reality which nevertheless affects a large proportion of us. The effects of racism, institutionalised and otherwise, can contribute to and exacerbate ill effects on health, and its operation should be seen as an implicit factor in all other areas of this book. But it is also important to look specifically at how racism can affect the health of children in a more explicit way.

The effects of racism on health are extremely disturbing.

A home should provide protection from hazards. It should be a safe, secure environment, somewhere that allows people to grow and develop.

For some this is not the case. Many people are fearful of walking the streets due to risk of assault but they can also feel threatened in their own homes. Racist graffiti daubed on walls, firebombs through letterboxes, bricks through windows, are becoming all too common.

Though extremely resilient, children may manifest the effects of such a stressful lifestyle through behavioural and emotional difficulties and stress-related illnesses.

Local authority housing departments often do not know how, or are unwilling, to handle these problems and may allow racist allocation policies to continue rather than face the realities of the situation.

Several studies (48,49,50,51) have shown that disproportionate numbers of black and ethnic minority families are living in the worst housing, particularly in the inner cities. They are frequently allocated accommodation in the worst state of repair - infested, damp, depressing. All these factors are shown to contribute to ill-health.

Black families and families from ethnic minorities are also disproportionately represented among the homeless and remain homeless longer (52) and are therefore exposed to the increased risks to health associated with this type of lifestyle.

The racist abuse of 'intentionality' and 'local connection' in Part III Housing (Homeless Persons) Act 1985 can also contrive to keep a disproportionate number of black and ethnic minority families in poor housing longer or even permanently.

A 1984 census estimated that there are 10,000 travelling families in Britain with up to 30,000 children under the age of 16 (53).

The lifestyle of travellers is becoming increasingly problematic. Changes in legislation have made it more difficult to find official sites. Along with the stress this causes, families may be forced to use sites without proper and adequate facilities.

One particular study (54) has shown that 33% of families lived on sites with no toilets, 14% with no baths or mains water or facilities which are dirty or unsafe. In addition, 39% of mothers felt sites were unsafe due to dirt, traffic, overcrowding, rat infestation and lack of safe play areas.

Some families have presented as homeless, unable to cope with the lifestyle any longer, only to find hotel life just as difficult.

Most health authorities are unaware of the numbers of travellers in their area and their needs are not taken into account when planning services.

While families are mobile, access to services is often difficult. Problems registering with GPs (54) and limited access to preventative services such as health visitors (55,56) can lead to a lack of follow up for children. As a result, there is little consistent care for children with chronic conditions and immunisation and developmental assessment may be delayed.

This is particular disturbing in the light of a study showing above average rates of low birthweight and perinatal mortality among travelling families (54).

Travellers also have to contend with racism due to ignorance about their lifestyle. The stress this causes as well as the fear of physical attack can have detrimental effects on families' health.

## SOME POSITIVE INITIATIVES

In East Anglia and Sheffield, the Save the Children Fund runs mobile clinics to provide accessible and appropriate health care for travellers.

A specialist health visitor for travellers is provided for the London boroughs of Hackney, Tower Hamlets and Islington. And in Sheffield, a clinical medical officer regularly visits sites with the health visitor.

There are no reliable figures on runaways but in 1985, 869 children under 14 and 2,113 14-17 year olds were reported missing in the Metropolitan police areas alone - the tip of the iceberg (57).

Whatever their reasons for leaving home, runaways then have to contend with life on the street, sleeping on friends' floors or, more rarely, with hostel or refuge life.

Homelessness is common among this group and all the problems that go with it.

The younger the child, the less likely they are to use hostels for fear of being sent home. Living on the street is very rough, even if it's for only a short period. Children will have no official means of claiming money so will have to turn to other avenues for income, such as stealing, prostitution, errand-running; they are constantly at risk of exploitation and violence.

This lifestyle also leads to increased health problems. Children who become ill may stay ill for long periods with no access to health care and with living conditions hardly conducive to healing. They commonly experience hypothermia, untreated injuries, malnutrition and increased infectious diseases (58).

It is already obvious from this report that research carried out into the effects of homelessness and poor housing on children's health makes for worrying reading.

In the 1980s, there are children who are still living in conditions that are making them ill or in some cases, contributing to their deaths.

Can we allow this to continue? Are we not being criminally negligent in allowing or causing the suffering of children in this way?

For too long, the effects of poor housing on children's health have been left in the background. The issues need to be further investigated and more fully understood AND taken into account in all central and local government decisions.

The answer is not simply to discover which houses are damp or falling apart and then repair them but to look in the long term at practices which would ensure that such conditions are not perpetuated.

We need to examine the relationship between income, deprivation, housing and health and to find practices which contribute to positive good health for all children.

Public health laws introduced in the last century are not safeguarding children's health. It is time to review those laws and reassess standards.

It would be easy to despair after reading some of the research to date into the effects of poor housing on children's health but we cannot afford to do that for the sake of their future.

The long term effects of poor housing are not yet fully understood - we must remedy that - but we already know too much to allow this situation to continue. We must begin to work now in a positive way to provide children with a better start in life.

*"Until these families can be housed adequately, any efforts to provide health care can only be seen in terms of a palliative."*

■

Health Visitor, Speaking for Ourselves, Bayswater Project

Out of the issues discussed in this report could come hundreds of specific recommendations. We could list them; agencies could ignore them. Agencies need to make their own lists, formulate firm policies and act upon them.

They need to look at the particular risks that children are facing in their areas and work towards eliminating those risks.

Policies need to be changed so that children and their families are no longer allowed to live in unacceptable conditions. Policies and practices need to be flexible so that each individual child can claim their right to live in good quality, appropriate accommodation.

*All agencies must put children first. Each adult should be an advocate for every child. Children rely on us to put their best interests first. We know that this would happen only in an ideal world but haven't children got a right to expect that we aim for that?*

Agencies must start talking to each other; children's health and housing status are so closely interlinked that each cannot pass responsibility onto others.

It is time to give children a better start in life by eliminating poor housing as a contributory factor in their ill health.

There must be:
■ improved liaison and collaboration between health, social services, housing and voluntary agencies at all levels
■ central government commitment to making children's health a priority. Funding should be made available to multi-disciplinary groups which can ensure this is the case in all housing policies, both at parliamentary and local levels. Joint funding should also be made available to health and local authorities to ensure good planning and management of housing
■ funds made available from central government for new house building and comprehensive repairs where appropriate to meet the immediate needs of those children living in poor housing
■ a commitment to new housing designed with all aspects of children's development in mind. Parents and the children themselves should be consulted. In planning new buildings, attention should be paid to wider external environmental factors such as the position of roads and volume of traffic or the situation of nuclear power stations
■ appropriate housing made available for children with special needs
■ housing policies which do not discriminate against the health of any child, whatever their race, age or social status and which take specific account of their particular needs
■ research initiated by central government to look at the long term effects of housing on children's health.

Finally, housing need should once again become a major public health issue. Health concerns must be central to all housing policy.

*"CHILDREN HAVE THE RIGHT TO AN ADEQUATE STANDARD OF LIVING. Every child has the right to benefit from an adequate standard of living. Parents have the primary responsibility to secure this but the states too have a role to play, particularly in ensuring that children are adequately nourished, clothed and housed."*

■

UNICEF, Convention on Rights of the Child, 1988

# SOURCES

1) Tars Folmer Andersen; Persistence of social and health problems in the welfare State - a Danish cohort experience from 1948-78; University of Copenhagen, Soc. Sci. Med. Vol 18 1984

2) N Britten, J Davies & J Colley; Early respiratory experience and subsequent cough and peak flow rate in 36 year old men and women, British Medical Journal, May 1987.

3) Anthea Holme; Housing and young families in East London;(reports of the Institute of Community Studies) 1985

4) Morris Schaefer; Health principles and housing; World Health Journal July 1987

5) Faith in the City; report of an Archbishop of Canterbury Commission on Urban Poverty Areas 1986

6) The Black Report - Inequalities in Health ; report of a research working group, DHSS 1980

7) Investing in the future - child health ten years after the Court Report; National Childrens Bureau 1987

8) Whitehead Report - Health Divide, 1987

9) E Taylor; 'Are there any clues to spot an at risk baby'; Pulse 1986

10) Steve Morton; specialist in housing, Faculty of Community Medicine; Radical Community Medicine, Spring 1988

11) Board of Science and Education; Deprivation and Ill-health, 1987

12) Rutter and Madge; Cycles of Deprivation, 1981

13) H L Freeman; Mental Health and the Environment 1985

14) P Elton M.F.C.M.; a community medicine specialist, North Manchester Health Authority; The effects of housing on mental health.

15) Dr Sonja Hunt with J Platt and C Martin 1988; Housing conditions and ill health, Edinburgh University

16) Strachman; House environment and respiratory morbidity in children, 1984

17) ML Burr, J Mullins, T Merrett, N Stott; Asthma and indoor mould exposure, 1985

18) H Hosen; Moulds in allergy, Journal of Asthma and Respiratory, Vol.15 1978

19) S Hunt, University of Edinburgh research unit in health and behavioural change; Health and Housing conference 1988

20) McCarthy et al; Respiratory conditions: effects of housing and other factors, 1985

21) Department of the Environment; An investigation of difficult to let housing, 1981

22) Alan Russell; The fight against the use of dangerous chemicals, Radical Community Medicine, Spring 1988

23) Shelter, SHAC, Maternity Alliance, London Food Commission; Prescription for poor health, 1988

24) Dr Sue Jenkins, Community Paediatric Research Unit; Homeless families in Bayswater - health and health services, 1987

25) Brennan and Lancashire; Association of childhood mortality with housing and unemployment, 1978

26) Herzog, Levy and Verdon; Ecological factors associated with health and social adaptation in city of Rotterdam, 1976

27) P Townsend, Phillimore and Beatie; Health and deprivation inequality and the north, 1987

28) Dr Jenny Morris; Disabled households in Tower Hamlets - Action for Disability, 1988

29) Department of Environment; Reducing vandalism on public housing estates, 1984

30) Tony Chiltern, Principal Children's Play Development Officer; Making the city fit the child, 1985

31) Nic Nilsson; Children's play needs are international, 1985

32) Magdalen Page, Bsc, Msc, Child Accident Prevention Trust; Child Safety and Housing, 1986

33) Pamela Constantinidies; Safe at Home, Radical Community Medicine, 1988

34) P Constantinidies and G Walker; Accidents and inequality in a London borough, 1986

35) Department of Environment figures; Health Visitor Journal, 1986

36) Valerie Howarth, Thomas Coram Foundation for Children; Survey of families in bed and breakfast hotels, 1987

37) Health Visitors Association/Shelter Survey 1986

38) Child Accident Prevention Trust, Child Safety and Housing;Home Accident Surveillance System, 1983

39) Dr Mumby; Allergy Handbook, 1988

40) Monica Brimacombe; Toxic Treatments, Roof May + June 1987

41) Childright; The Danger Overhead, 1986

42) David McLoughlin, Save the Children Fund; Homeless families in B&B, report to the director of child care, 1984

43) Sharon Richman and Dr Lessaeur; Department of Community Medicine, Parkside Health Authority, 1989

44) Steve Morton; Homeless families in Manchester, Faculty of Community Medicine 1988

45) Skrimshire; Area disadvantage - social class and health service, 1978

46) West and Lowe; Regional variations in need for and use of child health services in England and Wales, British Medical Journal, 1976

47) Prof. Neville Butler; Child Health and Education Study, Bristol, 1970s

48) Deborah Phillips; What price equality, 1985

49) Home Affairs Committee; Bangladeshis in Britain; HMSO 1986

50) Tower Hamlets Association for Racial Equality's response to Bangladeshis in Britain; Action Tower Hamlets 1987

51) Migrant Service Unit, London Voluntary Service Council; Migrants - The Invisible Homeless, 1987

52) Council for Racial Equality, Non-Discrimination Notice to London Borough of Tower Hamlets, 1987

53) Department of the Environment Census, 1984

54) Jan Pahl and Michael Vaile; Health and health care among travellers, Health Services Research Unit, University of Kent, 1986

55) Sampston and Stockford; Gypsy children and their health needs, Save the Children, 1979

56) Silver; Perinatal health and the traveller community, University of London, 1982

57) National Children's Home; Children in Danger, 1988

58)Erica De'ath; Inside the world of runaways, Community Care number 5 , February 1987